KEKI N. DARUWALLA is one of India's foremost poets and writers. His ten volumes of poetry include *Under Orion*, *The Keeper of the Dead* (winner of the Sahitya Akademi Award, 1984), *Landscapes* (winner of the Commonwealth Poetry Award, Asia, 1987), *Night River* and *The Map-maker*. His first novel, For *Pepper and Christ*, was shortlisted for the Commonwealth Fiction Prize in 2010. He was awarded the Padma Shri in 2014. Most recently, he was honoured with the Poet Laureate award at the Tata Literature Live! Mumbai Litfest, 2017. His work has been translated into Spanish, Swedish, Magyar, German and Russian.

Naishapur and Babylon

POEMS (2005-2017)

Keki Daruwalla

SPEAKING TIGER

SPEAKING TIGER PUBLISHING PVT. LTD
4381/4, Ansari Road, Daryaganj
New Delhi 110002

Published by Speaking Tiger in paperback 2018

Copyright © Keki N. Daruwalla 2018
Introduction copyright © Arundhathi Subramaniam

ISBN: 978-93-87164-10-9
eISBN: 978-93-87164-08-6

10 9 8 7 6 5 4 3 2 1

Typeset in Goudy Old Style by SÜRYA, New Delhi
Printed at Sanat Printers, Kundli

All rights reserved.
No part of this publication may be reproduced,
transmitted, or stored in a retrieval system,
in any form or by any means, electronic,
mechanical, photocopying, recording
or otherwise, without the prior
permission of the publisher.

This book is sold subject to the condition that it shall not,
by way of trade or otherwise, be lent, resold,
hired out, or otherwise circulated, without the
publisher's prior consent, in any form of
binding or cover other than that in
which it is published.

For Arundhathi Subramaniam

Whether at Naishapur or Babylon,
Whether the cup with sweet or bitter run,
The wine of life keeps oozing drop by drop,
The leaves of life keep falling one by one.

—Omar Khayyam (tr. Edward Fitzgerald)

CONTENTS

Introduction by Arundhathi Subramaniam   11

NAISHAPUR AND BABYLON

  What Lights Up...?   21
  In Night Country   23
  Naropa's Wife   25
  A Ram Kumar Painting on Benares   26
  Rain   27
  Cranes   29
  A Travel Book on Tibet   31
  At a Gompa in Bhutan   33
  Barbet   34
  A Daughter Speaks of the Great Brownings   35
  Letter   37
  Alhambra   39
  I Saw No Watchtowers   40
  Hieroglyph   41
  Ishtar   42
  Anaheita   43
  Dreams   44
  Lady By the River   46
  Still Life   48
  Colour   49
  The Knock   51
  Reverberations   52
  The Maid of Orleans   53
  On Re-reading Doctor Zhivago   54
  Some Poems for Akhmatova   55
  In Voronezh   58
  The Closed Glass Window   59
  Sleep Lands Securely   60
  Guide   61
  Patna to Nalanda—1979   62
  Cabral   63

River	66
Face	68
Migration 3	69
He Is Not Aware	70
She Came	71
A December Poem	72
She Talks of Sheshnag	73
The Tribal Goddess	74
A Dam in the Himalayas	75
The Confused Falcon	76
This Poem Is Going Nowhere Nor Is Life	77
I Wrote a Story	79
Prayer on January 30	80
Gandhi	82
Birds and Trees in Iraq	84
On a Bed of Rice	85

ORPHEUS AND PERSEPHONE

The Guard to Creon	91
Tiresias to Creon	92
Afterthought at Thebes	93
Greek Vases	94
Orpheus and Persephone	95

LUXOR DIARY

Small Truths	101
Rameses 111	102
The Ibis-god	103
The Temple to Hathor	104

TRANSLATIONS FROM FAIZ AHMED FAIZ

The Sad City	109
A Ghazal in the Memory of Makhdoom	110
Quatrains	111

Acknowledgements   113

Introduction

They say that mariners presage a storm by the way the skies behave. And that old farmer's almanacs anticipate the rains by the way the sun behaves. When I'm around the poetry of Keki Daruwalla, I take my cues from the way the birds behave.

The hawk, the eagle and the falcon have long been the imprimatur of Daruwalla's poetry, their restless wing-beat syncopating with his vigorous verse rhythms over the years. A keen observer and celebrant of the natural world, Daruwalla explores diverse historical and cultural contexts primarily through landscape, invoking it with expansiveness and exactitude.

It is his remarkable dexterity and economy of image that has always drawn me to his work. And the image is, I am aware, through my own practice, far more multivalent than the author's intention. So, I decided to allow the throb of the natural world, rich and instinct with life, to lead me through this diverse compilation of fifteen years of poetry.

That meant following the birds. It meant listening for the distant strains of birdcall, tracking changing patterns of migration, and waiting for a magical sighting of a heron's underbelly or a flash of hawk plumage. As a readerly strategy, it proved rewarding.

The raptors still soar high over Daruwalla's verse. But something has changed.

For one, the season is now often winter. And the temperature is at times Siberian. The landscape stays wooded and mountainous, river-incised, the winds still redolent with the scent of medieval voyages, of Egyptian antiquity and Aegean myth. Daruwalla's canvas is usually the great outdoors, panoramic vistas of mountain and steppe, giddy precipice and ocean, often Himalayan, Central Asian or Greek, viewed through the prism of a historical imagination. That has not changed. But dusk and night cast their shadows more often than before.

The birds remain plentiful and varied: the white heron, the kingfisher, the blue jay, the Himalayan thrush, the barbet 'like a caesura at the end of a long musical note'. But the birds themselves seem less predatory, less conquistadorial. Rather than the bird of prey looking down 'from the precipice of light', or the 'rapist in the harem of the sky', we are now offered a more contemplative feathered pageant: the owl in sync with human dreams, the perfection of 'the blue jay on the margosa tree', the crane with 'eyes closed in winged meditation', the snow eagle 'sedate as a lama'.

Time has most definitely changed too. More cyclical now, the wild hawk-king that once rode 'an ascending wind' begins to 'wheel', provoking 'circular meditations' on mortality, on beginnings and endings.

The great aerial sweep of gaze and expanse of pinion—or the impulse to adopt a bird's eye view of civilization and geography, as it were—endures. But older mysteries begin to reassert themselves, and these seem to require an approach more in alignment with gravity than in defiance of it. While Daruwalla is most certainly no mystic poet of inner realms, there is a greater willingness to acknowledge the secrets of the subterranean, the fathomless depths of sunken realms.

These secrets will not yield to demand. To understand 'the river's endless dreaming', one needs another approach—more watchful, more patient, more nocturnal. Here 'secrecy is another name for darkness'. This is 'night country' through which one finds one's way through attunement rather than conquest, through delirium rather than imperium. The old maps will not work here. This is a land that can unravel only through 'dream meditation'. And if the terrain is different, the 'map-maker' (the title of Daruwalla's ninth book of verse) must now turn explorer with a different set of tools. Tools of receptivity and illumination rather than initiative and assertion, seem to be called for. For as 'you go down', says the poet, 'you need a pine torch, you need an incense burner'.

It is with these implements of night vision that the deeper revelations may be garnered. What these are we do not yet know. But the sudden flash of kinship with the 'topaz-coloured eyes' of bear and deer 'glowing in the forest dark', just might have something to do with it.

And as attunement grows important, so does mutuality, which the poems seem to recognize as the basis of a more profound harmony. This produces several startling images. There is the reciprocity between sleeper and an owl 'rummaging among the rafters', who synchronize their nocturnal biorhythms. While the owl listens close to the sleeper's dreams, the sleeper keeps an ear open for 'the stir and hoot of its thoughts' all night. 'And so...' the speaker says, 'the forest and I kept watch over each other.'

There is also the senile old storyteller who lives in 'intricate harmony' with the world around him: 'with tide and tilted casuarinas and crabs,/ with dusk and salt sprayed over the road'. The poems seem to realize that these invisible ecosystems need acknowledgment, but also shamanic witness and protection.

Interestingly, most of the shamanic presences in this book are female. Since the topography has changed, a new mythology seems to be necessary as well. Figuratively, it would appear that Daruwalla's birds are now in quest of a new Simurgh.

Journeys have always been an important trope in Daruwalla's work. This persists. There is the surf-spangled voyage of that Portuguese 'bohemian of the sea', Pedro Cabral, for instance, tossed by the tides of adventure, 'carrying the load of our unknowings'. There is the fraught modern migration of a labourer from 'the wilderness of drought' to the 'city wilderness' of cement, concrete mixers and brick kilns. There is also the migration of the flooding river into urban 'hut and hamlet' (witnessed by a dazed dislocated family, a 'shaggy dog' and a calf, 'its halter rope trailing from the neck').

But among all the migrations is an even more ancient story of exile. More than one poem in the book underscores the banishment of the Divine Feminine to the underworld by 'the long-bearded messiahs' of patriarchal faiths. Accompanying it is a lament for the erasure of plural pagan traditions by the uncompromising severity of monotheism.

The Goddess recurs more than once, and in various avatars, in this volume. There is the 'grain-giver, barley goddess, goddess of word and melody', there is the 'moss-masked' goddess, the goddess 'of the dark heart of the forest', 'the vegetal goddess' and 'goddess of the watersprings still hidden in the earth'.

The only way to return to the realm of the goddess, tellingly, is through the night. And surely it isn't coincidental that an entire poem cycle is devoted to Persephone, who understands the dual logic of nether world and overworld like none other. For Tiresias, the blind seer, 'divination descends from the gods on high'. But for Persephone, wisdom is garnered from an understanding of sky and earth, from the ancient seasonal and vegetal cycles, older agrarian rhythms.

The unfortunate implications of the exile of the goddess from the human world are to be found on the terrestrial level as well. In a dramatic monologue by the wife of Tibetan mystic, Naropa, the irony is evident. While the husband is canonized for posterity, the wife is compelled to take 'the goat track to solitude'—and eternal anonymity.

As we are directed time and again to 'under' than 'over', we also seem to be reminded that our ideas of home will have to change. While the aerial images of beauty are still discernible, there are several reiterations of roots as a deeper source of nourishment. The language of poetry seems to find more profound mainsprings here—in this world where hieroglyphs are 'roots into the unwritten dark'.

Not surprisingly, the tree—whether of 'life', of 'time, of 'signs', or of 'knowledge'—is also a recurrent presence in this book. With it comes the symbolic reminder of the tree of world myth that unites sky and earth, night and day, birth and death. Reminiscent of the Indian banyan, the Zoroastrian Haoma tree, the Norse Yggdrasil, it seems to remind us that the hawk of Daruwalla's verse might now be in quest of another kind of eyrie.

A sense of loss is pervasive. But the dominant mood is not melancholic. There is a very real acknowledgement of what terminations might mean: when a wife, for instance, drives off in a dream in 'our blue Standard Herald', the speaker remarks with quiet understatement, 'I said I'd wait for lunch/ and I waited and waited/ and then it struck me/ she wasn't coming back'.

A robustness of spirit remains. And there is gratitude. It is evident in several poems, including the paean of praise to colour that ends with a caveat: 'We thank you for colour, Lord,/ and lest I forget/ we thank you for the eye'.

The silent landscape seems to offer its own consolations. This is definitely not spring, but there is beauty to be discerned in the 'thin winter cry of a Himalayan thrush'. This is not 'the time for the oxen and the plough', but it is not the time for 'elegy' either. Besides, 'absence' can turn 'companion', silence can be like 'loam, alive with snail and earth', and dream and darkness can be places of clarity. And when dream fails us, all is not lost, for even 'flatness' can be a kind of 'bliss', offering 'freedom from premonition' and 'the harsh light of clairvoyance'. Above all, there is joy of a kind in having no more 'cliffs to ascend', 'no precipice' to keel over.

Particularly interesting is the preoccupation with time. It is not the march of history and civilizations, or the Biblical 'time of the flood and the ark' that interests Daruwalla in this book. Nor is it time in deep-freeze—'entombed', 'frozen' or 'drugged'. When pioneering seafarer Pedro Cabral thanks God that he isn't an Indian obsessed with the inner life, looking 'for every answer in the oceans of the self', Daruwalla is clearly taking a rueful jibe at his own cultural location. The poet is aware that every historical epoch, like every individual, has 'its interiors, secrets, anxieties, silences', that every epic adventure outward is not without its own ambiguities.

And when temporality meets artistry, we see time for what it is ultimately capable of: a radical state of the present continuous. The Alhambra therefore is a dream that never really 'happened'. But in a beautiful companion poem, it is 'always happening'. As architecture is transmuted by creativity into a state of exquisite continuum, place becomes process, marble becomes life, and eternity is now.

Things may be darker in a book that Daruwalla describes as his last volume of poems. But the apocalypse is not here yet. Far from it. Things do not fall apart. And the relationship between the falcon and the falconer isn't a problem. If anything, the bird simply realizes it now needs other skills—the capacity to soar *and* to fall, to rise *and* to swoop. The falcon seems, in fact, to acquire a keener intelligence as it learns to respect gravity.

There are pleasures in reaching the highest branch of the tree, but there are pleasures too, the poet suggests, in exploring the 'dark crypt of our psyche', or diving to reach the 'word-leaf' in its 'never-ending fall from the tree of knowledge'. There is a time to extend wing and annex the skies, but wisdom also in recognizing when to be as 'quiet as a falcon on the winter's wrist', or a barbet hidden deep 'in the tree of time'.

Daruwalla's verbs have lost none of their feral quality. His poetic line remains, for the most part, sinewy and energetic. The capacity to combine atmospheric sweep with succinctness, and to turn out the startling turn of phrase with an almost throwaway air are unchanged. Several moments in these poems linger long after one has closed the book: the wind 'whetting its razor on eroded slopes', 'leaves like old scrolls wrapped in their crackling selves', 'a firefly pulsing/low on battery', 'the full-throated tremolo [of wolves] ricocheting in the wilds', 'the tangled reed-and-sedge locks of Shiva', and 'elegy moving like a slow Wagnerian movement', to name just a few. Clearly, the 'streak of fire' that courses through 'the thin wire of memory and mind' is alive and well.

There are reiterations, as before, of the capacity of art to embody a truth deeper than a daylight world of fact. The Persian poet Firdausi in Daruwalla's previous book, *Fire Altar*, puts it memorably: you may 'invent as much as you chronicle', he says, but 'a people's past is only safe with bards'. The sentiment is echoed in this volume as well. 'But reflections are the real thing, aren't they,' the poet asks here at one point. And when he writes about 'the birds and trees' in Iraq, we realize that the reflections are, in fact, far more revealing than any newspaper headline or statistic. For the kingfisher that flutters over the river Tigris leaves in its wake 'a warped image' that 'struggles and shivers' in the water. That distorted, struggling image is a more profound testimony to truth than any political slogan.

And yet, in a book where attunement is the key word, there are alternative images of art as well—truer than fact, and yet, integrally wedded to life. The relationship between art and life now seems less binary, less oppositional. In the enchanted core of the universe, nature meets culture effortlessly—as effortlessly as light meets shadow, and lovers meet the muse; as inevitably as hallucination meets fact, river meets mythology, water meets mist and memory, art meets alluvium, and star meets song.

'Let the forest leaf, let the lyric leaf', the poet says in a moment of benediction. In this heart of existence, life, it would seem, is gracefully alchemical. It is perfectly natural here for 'the dripping deciduous word-leaf' to fall off the tree of life and morph into a lyric—and perfectly natural too for a haiku to turn into a bird and fly off a page.

The birds may be migrating towards newer myths. But their gaze remains keen, their wing span formidable. Vigorous and powerful, the poems of Keki Daruwalla continue to take wing.

Arundhathi Subramaniam

Naishapur and Babylon

What Lights Up...?

what lights up
    the light-bulb filaments
of your recall Old Man
this streak of fire
through the thin wire
    of memory and mind
        what line
            from which poet?

the ibex looking down
    quizzically
at our car from cliff
the croc sunning corrugated hide
on the banks of the Rapti
as I cross the river rolling on elephant back
    wary elephant treating river-bed like a mine
trundling diagonal across the current

and red-robed monk
    slowing down life not through *asanas*,
    but with mumbled prayer
that slow-rolls the cylindrical prayer drum;
and stars
    at their night shift
in Ladakh

I don't remember the dripping
    deciduous word-leaf
        holistic-halfway-through
           its never-ending
             fall
from the tree of knowledge

and your eyes I remember them
    bright as a window of a just-lit room
    seen from the cinder-dark
        outside
the black-moment cinder-dark
that was I at that moment

sad isn't it
    (not a bit)
the spyglass getting hazed
    in the cold
as it peeps into the mist and melancholy
of the gone-by *guzishta*,
Urdu word for the past,
memory sabotaging memory
past subverting past.

Note: This poem was written after a query at the end of a Himalayan car safari lasting 78 days.

In Night Country

She is so ephemeral
she is ephemera herself
alights
    for a precipitous moment
    on nerve-edge
        dream-edge,
dream that darkens into a forest
where only shadows thrive

steps
    for one luminous moment
    on that rim
        where consciousness and amnesia
    meet and vanish
    blur and meet

she has almost become invisible
the plough can't reach her under the furrow
though dealers in the occult
    have seen her image
        splash for a moment in deep wells.

2

When you are neglected for three millennia
you retire underground
    one with the seedling's
    long night of germination

    long-bearded messiahs
drove you under the earth—
    the ones who thought they had a direct line
        to Him, the maker of planets,
            marker of orbits,

a hot line to the manufacturer of stars.
      they hadn't heard
of black holes, comets and quasars
or these too would be in our scriptures.

3

Groves were sacred to her, they say
now axe and saw mill work overtime there

old bards, high
on hash and cannabis
could lasso her with an incantation;
    but old bards are gone
        and so is their music

some lucky ones have heard your silks rustle
(the hem always beyond reach)
    they haven't seen you, unsure
        if that wasn't the wind in the cedars

a sibyl once said it's not
that She won't reveal herself
it's that they are
    afraid of her revelation.

4

Yet as the year waxes and the dying winter
moves past the thaw ooze
we find her voice in the songbird's throat;
at dusk in lapwing country,
the cacophonic lapwing country,
    one senses her presence.
and somewhere in a dark crypt of our psyche
unknown to ourselves
there is a small hooded flame
that belongs to her, she, grain-giver
barley-goddess, goddess of word and melody.

Naropa's Wife

I never heard of the soul's call
not even when I married him at sixteen.
Bird calls and the call of the heart, yes,
but not this.

Eight years he revelled in my body and my love
then I noticed his heart or was it his soul (?)
(am getting confused) withdrawing.
I could feel the spasms of his coiled silences.
the call of a no-where-nirvana
got to him, and the call of the ochre dust
not bits like the prayer wheel, but meditation,
      trance, dharma, penance:
dangerous words all.

One day he said 'I must leave'.
I was used to his talk of ephemera and illusion—
the two words tangled in such a knot
that I didn't know which was which—
'I will say to the world' he went on
that women only beguile
    they are swamp, deception.'
when he spoke these very words to our parents,
I echoed him.
He was preaching, not making excuses(!)
'illusion' and 'ephemera' walked in again, as ever.
I lowered my head and said I was worthless.

He took the road
I took the goat track to solitude.
But my solitude was not ephemera.

Note: Naropa (1016-1100), one of the most revered saints of Tibetan Buddhism, was born in Bengal. His marriage was dissolved by mutual consent in 1040, the year he went to Kashmir. The wife's name, as preserved in Tibetan scriptures, is Ni-gu-ma.

A Ram Kumar Painting on Benares*

Night has smeared itself on this landscape, Ram Kumar
and so have dream and sadness.
As a stillness rests on river and city,
the oblongs your abstract brush have left
get half-lit—they throb, though their
river-reflections are indistinct.

But reflections are the real thing,
aren't they Ram Kumar?
and you missed out on those
for isn't Benares a parasite on the river,
that torrent of myth which inundates the country?

This is a nocturne on Benares
sound lowered, its silence
that of an underground pool

all movement is frozen in dream;
pilgrim, mourner, ochre and anchorite
even the starscape nudged out of the canvas.

The ghats are in a trance now
brass bells meditate on silence, temple-spires
on their inverted cones in the current
but on your canvas a half light
trembles on the absence of reflections.

---

*Varanasi, oil on canvas, 50" x 70", 1966

Rain

    is memory
each string of water
as it sheets down
    in murk and mist,
        soft-spearing the earth,
    excavates the steam
    buried in the planet,
        and comes out with
    tuber memory.

memory
    is Matheran
where on the first day
of the window-lashed
and shutter-banging wind,
as the rain comes down
like a lake overturned in the skies,
        lightning breaks its back
        upon the ramparts
        and I think of father
eloquent on the ghats
and Shivaji and Matheran.

rain
on the brick-ochre tiles
    sounds different,
has a smothered ring
    about it
so different from
the rafters in Kashmir
        where the night rain clicks away
and sleep gets spattered
by dream and rain and sound

and the birds are different
    and the droplets on their wings
    have a different tint
as they slide down and lose colour
and the magpie robin is silent
and so is the spotted owl
as they tuck their beaks
within wing and down
and wait and wait
for the rain to end
even as I wait for the next
bit of memory
    and fail to find it.

Cranes

they came
in a black cloud
    from tibet
flying horizontal
over freezing flats
    eyes closed in
winged meditation.
year after year they came
    on the same
day prefacing winter;
lifting themselves slowly
nudged by an instinct
buried in the glands
    before alighting
on the ridged valley
of gangtey,
    dream-dark.

the calendar was
no mystery to them
    air current, wind-drifts
were familiar friends,
knew them better
    than fish know
the rhythm of tides;
sensed kinship with
    the valley, for this is
a vale of compassion
      where none is harmed

as winter lopes along
tableland and mountain,
    bird speech crowds this
vale of cypress and hemlock;
then people mourn as spring
    draws near, for now the
crane-cloud lifts to move north
over cairn and gompa,
    like a black halo.

Note: The black-necked cranes fly from Tibet to the Gangtey valley in Bhutan from October 23rd to 26th every year and return in February. The poet was there on October 18 and 19.

A Travel Book on Tibet

has tsampa and yak dung-smoke on adobe walls
snow storm without and laughter within adobe walls

has prayer wheels on the outer verandahs
and butter lamps souring on lacquered tables

has demons and other spirits on gompa walls
you can't make out the decent from the bad.

The wheel of existence will be everywhere
you too will bow, for the travel author has knelt there.

The earlier you learn of wheels and circularity,
and shun straight lines, the better for your arc of destiny.

A travel book on Tibet has a thinness of air about it
has a high-wheeling altitude

which Yeats could never have felt or thought of
in his gyres over Byzantium.

2

On a gompa wall I've known a Manchu archer
from Tartary, on a stylized horse, his back curving

as he fires his arrow to the rear, to the past.
A travel book on Tibet carries you to the past,

cleaving through the present, the ubiquitous Han,
quick music and gadgets, electricity and muscle;

it moves to old scrolls, where a red-robed Lama picks out
an ancient oracle's warning—how could it be so right (?)

in the ill-starred year of the Wood-Dragon
Tibet would face its first invasion from the south!*

But we must move beyond oracles, brother.
Good Lamas go further back, they move with the Buddha
travelling from one incarnation to another.

---

*Younghusband's expedition/attack in 1903 on Tibet was predicted. The medical officer of the expedition, Lt. Col Waddle, has recorded this in the history of the expedition

At a Gompa in Bhutan
(In the year of the Water Sheep)

cliff as backdrop
monastery in front
wooden façade,
corniced, carved, painted
gold on door and drum;
a sparrow hawk wheeling
harmless in an innocent sky
overseeing red robes
and tonsured heads.
snow eagle sitting on a wire
in the yard below
sedate as a lama.
flat drums
and the nine-foot trumpet
with three joints
have paid their hoarse compliments
to the arriving dignitary.

Barbet

Like a caesura, at the end of a long musical note
time finds its element in winter, stations itself
at the centre of things and non-things;
the texture of time and thought are the same—
not palpable to touch;

Winter is a time when time looks back
                while the landscape broods
time never broods—meditation is its other name;
it meditates on black bark, snowless winter
hibernation and polar bears,
and wind whetting its razor on eroded slopes.
time also hunkers down, thinking of absences,
(absence is a being after all, absences pulse, hide in corners, caves)
then time allows an intrusion in its trance—
the absence of the barbet and its concertina-throated call.

Winter is a time when time looks back
solitude takes a long lingering look at solitude,
absence turns companion;
fall after fall, winter after winter
the barbet and its call go missing
a bird-shadow current, warmed by the memory
of some distant summer, passes by, and from its
hidden hole in the tree of time the bird calls *kuraa kuraa*;
so much longing and hope in its two-word language.

Cold again and the tree hole silent
till the mango flower puts out its fluff
this time the call from its heavy red bill
is an octave lower—for it calls in retrospect.

A Daughter Speaks of the Great Brownings

Mother, quiet till dusk, would open up at night
when, alone with father's memories,
she'd say the stars didn't side with him,
but kept quiet when the zodiac
entered our house, bristling with sign and symbol.
I'd taken to astrology to find out
what happened to him, peer into
the layers of absences our mist was made of.

'Daughter, you turning sibyl!' she laughed one day,
'the future is a forest you'll get lost in.'
I couldn't tell her I was looking for the past.

The stars were quiet and never spoke to me.

Then I came upon this forest and told Ma we'd settle here,
and some day the stars in monologue mode, would perhaps open up.
I inhaled the night air and the night jar's call that never came through
and silence, like the loam, alive with snail and earthworm.
A low-slung moon, overhearing the low note
of its own light rustling through the foliage, gripped me.
We pitched our tent here, meaning we rented the house.

Wind, quiet as a falcon on the winter's wrist,
Light, the colour of unreflecting water,
Leaves, like old scrolls, wrapped in their crackling selves.

When night came four hours after noon,
the last spurt of life I saw was a chipmunk,
its tail flickering in the dry crackle of rust,
till it heard my look drilling through the glass,
raised its furred head and bolted
startled by a summons intuitively accessed.

For half the night the owl talked to itself.
We heard each other, it listened to my dreams
rummaging among the rafters.
I heard the stir and hoot of its thoughts
and saw the bulbs of its eyes switch on
with phosphorescence that lit up half the woods.
And through the first watch of the night
the forest and I kept watch over each other.

Letter

during these empty seasons
it is passé to survive
hence this letter out of nowhere to you
as if you were alive.
there are dreams to decipher at dawn
before you throw them in the bin,
the round of unlatching windows
to let the cool air in;
plucking a blade of lemon grass,
clean the gas-burner, kindle a fire-ring
to put the kettle on boil, sniffing hard
to find if there's some fragrance left in
this grass planted a year back in our yard.

newsprint comes in handy, and tea
rustle of headlines meaningless tomorrow;
the bustle of things going awry, except
the spin and orbit of astral spheres.
pigeons explode next, troubled by a noise
that hasn't reached my ears;
they circle round wall and hedge
settle back to shuffle on the wire
or leave birdlime on the ledge.

poetry? as one gets on in age
I write around the same dream
on the same page
paper gets larger, dream shorter.

our daughter tore a knee ligament
while skiing, happens I presume;
it's been surgically repaired
am not certain by whom.
as for news and notable events
I am not sure if there is much;
the day goes by; sold the old jalopy
some years back; we haven't kept in touch.

Alhambra

the flowering vines
red and yellow petalled
that fringe the battlements here
are not Alhambra
battlement and rampart themselves
are not Alhambra
calligraphy glowing on the tiles
is not Alhambra either—
it's black or sometimes gold
curves of the quill
are a hallucination of sorts
the script embossed
on a light-on-flowing water era,
all this is not Alhambra

fountains that shimmer and drape
the river palace in a veil of water
are not Alhambra
gardens imported from paradise
sprayed and spread-eagled
around the palace
are not Alhambra.
Alhambra is a dream resting
on the drugged eyelids of the planet,
on the eyes of drugged time.
seriously
Alhambra never happened.

I Saw No Watchtowers

I saw no watchtowers
over Alhambra
who needs poised spear
or arrow on the tense bowstring
when guarding beauty?

who needs
a matchlock-wielding *barqandaz*
to guard illusion?

Alhambra never happened
or perhaps,
the core of beauty in our lives
being what it is,
Alhambra is always happening.

Hieroglyph

don't throw me a hieroglyph
            to unravel
i won't be able to walk its timeless
                edge
i cannot dig my way
    to its entombed centre
its time is different
it's not the time of the flood and the ark
or the red sea splitting
    or the sack of yerushalayim
and the cold stiff silence of death
    around the wailing wall

hieroglyphs are roots into the unwritten dark.
Nabu had a dream, saw speech
    coded and coiled
            in the roots
of this tree of signs
Nabu, the Assyrian god
        saw cipher and symbol
    giving birth to script
    saw hieroglyphs as dreams
    that language dreamt
    before it was born

Ishtar

goddess,
        myth-clad
you were never really there
        in flesh and radiance
lion-enthroned.
for us Sumerians, Akkadians
        and people of Nineveh and Arbela
who bent the knee to you
you were a nerve in the mind
a vein in the body we tapped with prayer
        when lightning fell on the ziggurat
but left us without a burn.

yet you were everywhere
strolling down planet Venus
        and our lands between the two rivers,
lions flanking you.
        the night you knocked
at the underworld gates
        the doors wouldn't fly open
your threats boomed like thunder-echo
'open or I'll smash door and door post
and command the dead to rise and eat the living.'

at each of the seven gates of the nether world
        you shed a garment
autumn's yellow leaf and the brown of frost-mud,
drought and skeletal winter,
        symbol-garments all
falling from your lustrous shoulders.

now we bemoan the loss
   of the gate you disappeared with
   the Ishtar gate lighting up the old world
   with its glaze of lapis lazuli.

KEKI N. DARUWALLA

Anaheita

Even as I cleared the shaggy edge
    of the woods
so that sunlight could somehow
    dribble down to my garden,
I got this queer feeling
    that I had made it easier
for bear and deer to eye us,
their topaz-coloured eyes
    glowing in the forest dark.

Next morning, or was it
    the morning after that (?)
the deer came, four of them
and ate up the hydrangea
    and the astilbe,
but never touched the rhododendrons.
    Deer don't have a taste for rodis.

I was a bit aggrieved
    the deer hadn't belled
        before moving in
        and I shooed them off.

They'll come again, they always do
    the garden is within their cross hairs.
Now the roses and the delphinium
    await their second coming.

Dreams

Throughout my dreams
I am at different places,
seldom at home; but often
even when the place is strange
I think it is home.
Time and place get mingled—
the year may be a stranger
but I feel that we have met.
Then time switches on its
soul-conditioning plant
and I feel the draft;
it switches on its shadow-light,
I don't spot the borderline
between eras, yet I can sense
the rain of the past drumming
on the roof-tiles of the present.

***

Dream II

There's no nonsense about my dreams
I never have wings or even a car
I am never down and out, but anxious
that I could be down and out.
The train doesn't stop midway through the night
in fact I am never on the train
but waiting anxiously at the platform
and as far as I remember, the train never arrives.

The other day wife drove off
in our low slung car
our blue Standard Herald
which we had for twenty years.
I said I'd wait for lunch
and I waited and waited
and then it struck me
she wasn't coming back.

Lady By the River

She may not be beautiful but she's still serene
though she doesn't look into mirrors
                anymore
she spots herself
    in the jaw line
        and long eyelashes
            of her granddaughter.

She doesn't face mirrors anymore
but she looks into the river now and then
      the river which is so brown
that it takes an era
    for her reflection to sink in.

The boatman who has been ferrying her silks
            and her silken youth
    will not comment on her.
The village women say
she has stopped speaking to the boatman
    but she talks to the river.

                    ***

Lady By the Mist

She may not be beautiful but she's still serene
Her hair may not be black or silver
    but a remnant of lustre still glazes it.
The blue veins, once visible on her arms
           are lost these days
within the gradual darkening of her skin.
Flesh may have receded a little from her face
    but the bone doesn't show.

Her gaze is far seeing, eyes fixed on distance—
  (reminds me of binoculars
  forgotten on the bank).

Her long-lashed granddaughter
looks at her as if she is river-mist.

Still Life

Mud hut—woman at the door
shading her eyes against the morning sun.
Distance flowering yellow with mustard
rice straw drying
the blue jay brilliant on the margosa tree.

***

Still Life II

Mud hut—woman at the door
face grey as mud, hair scraggy as rice straw.
Heat above and around, wilted yellow below.
Absence of the blue jay heavy on the branch
fatigued old retina eyeing the world.

Colour

Lord
You have much to answer for.
You made these politicians.
and I could name a few
except that I am scared of slander suits
in our moderately corrupt courts—
must keep judges on the right side, Lord,
hence the moderate bit.

But you also made colours,
the after-rain morning that obliterates night,
a hundred shades of green
a hundred shades of Spring
which mean the same thing—I didn't wish to be ambiguous.
You made the cloud layers, the one
    with the thunder, black moisture-cloaked inside,
        moving into the grey one which itself
overlaps the cloud
    with the colour of
a white heron's underbelly.
You give those aquatints
    the white heron's image in the blue river
that could be the envy of a water colour artist,
gave us the cloud-shadow whose whisper
    the young wheat can hear
        but we can't.

One thing about colour, Lord,
these language-philosophers say,
that if a thing doesn't have a name to call it by, it doesn't exist.
But even without a name
colours would have registered themselves on the eye
    like a printout.

We thank you for colours, Lord
and lest I forget
we thank you for the eye.

The Knock

The wind knocks at your door
    and you let it in
Dry leaves scrape your door
    and you let them in.
If you were to ruminate
(if you ever had time
    for rumination, that is)
you'd feel for a fly-by moment
that a particular knock you heard
on the far edge of awareness
        was mine.

On the other hand you may never have heard
    a shadow's tenuous leaf-tap, muffled tap.
It was a harmless knock, I can tell you
—perhaps to meet and tear apart a solecism
or share a perfect iamb I had prised out
    of some crumbling book

But you were another island

The window and skylight of your airy house
    may have opened to a gust of rain,
to gnat and insect, even a firefly pulsing
        low on battery.
But you were so much in love with light
    you couldn't hear a shadow knock
    you wouldn't let a shadow in.

Reverberations

I am not sure what reverberates across continents
or those hairline borders pocked with dugouts
where we string barbed wire and put up sentry posts.
I know earthquakes vibrate and reverberate
and how(!), across line and street and I know
how tramlines warp and walls bend at the ankle.

If you are deaf to sounds and boasts
and advertising and have kept your voice low
through a lifetime, sounds turn interior,
and you hear all the while in your old age
the muted trumpet of your ego.

The Maid of Orleans

Any film on Jean d'Arc
will end on the stake,
sur le boucher, as the Burgundians,
who did her in, call it.
If the film is just about the trial—
disoriented rustic lady
shorn of hair,
abandoned by voices, visions,
facing clerics made to look
every inch like Mephistopheles,
best not to see it.

The camera and I are rustics
we can't identify Pierre Couchon,
Bishop of Beauvais who
set her up for heresy and the stake.
The fellow, despite his robes
could as well have been
a commandant at Treblinka.
She's not there on the ramparts,
a whirlwind behind her banner
hurling the English back.

The stake differs from film to film
but does it matter if she sizzles
in reed and faggot
or log and pinewood?
Belief, heresy and
clerical chicanery
are all a part of the blaze.
Look for the camera angles now
as flames billow up
dense and delirious
and credits ascend the screen
between smoke and starlight.

On Re-reading Doctor Zhivago

The wolves are not baying at the moon;
their snouts are pointed towards the house of love.
Around them the frost of the Siberian winter;
around them the snow and their reflections in the snow,
black charcoal strokes that stand out in the snow.
They obviously can't sense what is going on in the house
around candle flame, tallow flame, dimly lighting up the house,
the desperate birth of headlong desperate love.
They don't know the language in which poetry
is descending on him, they can't sense the love
surging in the two of them, have never known
if poetry is different from love or conjoined.
The lovers and the muse don't know this themselves,
and all that the wolves know at this star-lit snow-moment
is the half-whimper, long drawn howl, spearing upwards—
the full-throated tremolo ricocheting in the wilds—
snorkels raised at the Siberian winter which for them
stretches like a vast sidereal winter.
They are not baying at the black blood
drying on the dry leaf-loam of the Taiga;
they are not baying at the winter of the Revolution
that will snuff out the flame in that candle-lit house of love.

Some Poems for Akhmatova

1

You knew your eyes
were transparently radiant

You knew how to love
and to look into other's eyes

You were so slender
I thought you were as light as your curls

You were young
so was the century

But even as you talked of lilies,
their petals tremulous with dew

You walked the abyss with others
the abyss was always with you.

2

Where did this vein
of dark prophecy come from?

Ten years before the War
thirteen before the Revolution

you heard the wind's howl
ricocheting over the voids

and you saw or foresaw
a grave abandoned by its inhabitant,

the cross on the headstone gleaming
ghost-white in the phosphorescent air.

3

I have a poem like yours
the ewe talking of the shepherd
and his throwing stick
and her lamb being roasted
for the prodigal son.
Then I came upon your
"Invitation from the Armenian".
But your black ewe is addressing
the Padshah that was Stalin.

That upped the scales. My ewe
was only talking to the shepherd, the Lord.
Stalin was a different samovar of tea
altogether a bigger bowl of goulash.
What can the black ewe ask
now that the lamb is cooked, I wondered.
Yet I started sinking when you said to the walrus moustache
"Was he tasty my little son?
Did he please you, please your children?"
I sank—there are hearts which keep sinking
even after they hit the sea floor.

4

In the disgraced poet's room
Terror and poetry watch by turns
And night is switched on interminable;
At its taper-end no dawn will burn.

5

(To the Woman in the Prison Queue)

Woman with the blue lips
standing in the Leningrad cold,
bread queue, prison line?
Woman without a name
perhaps without bread
awaiting your turn
to see son, lover, frozen behind bars
as you turn blue under a frosty sky,
you are immortal in a way
despite the erasure of your name.

Your face stares out of her poem,
and your question, can you describe this:
hunger and air brittle with cold and fear (?)
and when Akhmatova agrees,
we watch the wintry smile trudging across
the memory of what once had been your face.

In Voronezh

(what happened to M. in the Lubianka during his interrogation?)

we sat together sifting hallucination
                from fact
not easy as you think
        for fever
and stabs of momentary delirium
still assaulted him
yet he saw my mother's coat on me,
and concluded
'so you haven't been arrested.'
the grains of the actual past
had to be carefully locked away,
        velvet-covered in a vault,
and partitioned
        from the things he imagined

(though what is grain
and what is chaff
is not for the likes of me to define)

there was a time we had met
the interrogator together
        I served as a phonograph disc there
the interrogator's voice, his alchemized
version of events, the altered past,
being recorded for meadow and moor
and echoes meant for the outside world

why must people think
        that reality can so easily
be translated?

The Closed Glass Window

the closed glass window
has the tree in its sights as it slowly undermines
        the outer wall.
there is no bird
but a birdcall lost in the morning
hangs on the cable-wire like a paper kite
        in spring, but this is not spring.
it's early evening, moist with no sun,
tucked nowhere between a nowhere autumn
        and the dying rains.
the glass bookcase
    reflects my face
in a half-blind half haze.
      hooked to words, boxed in,
I look for words in the room
echoes of hoped-for palpable
        responsive-to-touch words in the room
and for reality outside the window
 where the tree-root
slow as time, with the deliberation of time
        undermines my wall and me.

Sleep Lands Securely

sleep lands securely on the eye
fake helicopter
on fake helipad

nights dense with dreams:
seas that heave and blur and fade
to low tide and recession

fog-smeared walls; furniture, floors
that unpleat themselves, colour as always
deserting the night and dream

panels of vapour
the thumbprint of time
gets embossed on my vision

silence masks the landscape
and when there is speech
there's no identifiable speaker

flatness is bliss, no cliffs
to ascend, no precipice that drives down
to a seam of marble interned in time

hope this lasts, freedom
from premonition, nights that do not drift
into the harsh light of clairvoyance.

Guide

The guide, flown specially from Delhi,
caresses the smooth sandstone
and turns garrulous
as he shows us the elephant head.
A big Ashokan edict perhaps
lies waiting to be exhumed
from this debris of mud and sun-baked brick
that litters the land here.
He points out the minutiae;
the inverted lotus on the abacus—
lotus, mud-born and yet
rising above the mud,
foliate efflorescence,
the peepal leaf everywhere;
names the flying celestials
on a terracotta plaque;
knows his panels—
each rib and flange,
and the hectic fantasy of the apsaras.
The parrot perched on the shoulder
pecks her breast,
mistaking it for fruit.
And that canopy of the cobra-hood,
shading the Buddha's head
is the snake turned worshipper
after his poison turned harmless
in the Buddha's body.

A woman bows to his torrent of words.
'Why?' I ask bewildered.
Her smile is as benign as the Sakyamuni's.
'He knows as much about this holy statuary,
as the Buddha knew about the fate of souls!'

Patna to Nalanda—1979

time stalks the clock tower
in a circular prowl

sun beats down, the tarmac runs
along the radials of a sundial

bricks abound
to build a hugger mugger future

a half-brick converts
to the caste which holds it

used tyres, a past erased
on their de-treaded grooves

a cobbler under a spiked canopy
stitches his torn feet

water nuts effloresce into a bleached purple
women carry baskets bulging with aubergine

a two-foot temple at the foot of a banyan tree
the temple latticed by descending prop roots

astrologer searching for a lost horoscope
a bypass gets lost in the bowels of the city

mendicants wander in search of a thirst
thirsts come looking for a monastery

the cotton bow twangs
as it twanged in the days of the Buddha.

Cabral

We head east at last, the sails full
and gulls skimming over the wake,
till they find a claw-hold on the rigging.
We have left behind Vera Cruz and the natives,
copper-coloured, innocent and naked—
the naked are normally innocent.
The Franciscan Friars on my ship would be unhappy
to hear me speak thus, but they were friendly
enough (the friars I mean) to actually
adorn those brown necks with crucifixes.
The natives didn't know what a cross stood for,
but they were intrigued by the metal.

We move towards the southern tip of this land-spill
that is Africa, putting our faith in God
and Bartolomeu Dias, first in history
to have rounded the Cape. We're almost there.
Our spirits rise like yeast and then subside,
for first the wind rises, soughing like
a million beetles wheezing in unison;
clouds drape the skyline, and the waves blot it;
then the sea coils and storms up, recoils and falls
while rigging and mast turn frail as bird-bone.
Four ships go down, not mine though,
but Dias is now a skull on the seafloor.
The Cape of Good Hope we called it, of good hope!

2

We're not forging a new epoch and that's hard
for me to say, and for the rest to understand.
I look within—to the inner workings
of an outer bound era. I look for
light in the brown cave of solitude.
Does an era have interiors, secrets,
anxieties, silences? I can't answer that one.
Thank God I am no Indian, who looks
for every answer in the oceans of the self.

The next voyage on the first route garners no glory.
Bohemians of the sea, we wind-crawl, current-crawl
carrying the load of our unknowings;
worrying about barter: cruzados and cowries;
watching the frenzy of vegetation on the coasts,
and losing our way in the thickets of their language.
But even Swahili must have a word for sorrow
and one for love, and while about it
a word for mating, for after sundown and sin-fall
it is mating that's crucial, isn't it (?)
whatever those Platonists might say.

3

The silt of despair didn't weigh us down
though our mood was sombre as we struck north
for Sofala, axle and hub of the gold trade;
the harbour narrow, shoal and shingle mingled
to frighten the pilots. We moved
to Kilwa knowing that the place was hostile.
We received live goats and a boatload of food
from Sultan Ibrahim. A meeting was arranged
on a raft gaudily touched up. His musicians
blew on ivory horns, ours on trumpets.
I handed our King's letters, just two things he wanted—

a trade-post to get at Sofala's gold
and the people of Kilwa to give up Islam.
We need time said the Sultan, and the next day
I found it was not the Sultan we'd met
but an imposter! Who was it who said
'the twine of the East is hard to unravel.'
We waited two days, and when no answer came,
we demanded fresh water.

Boatloads arrived with water sloshing
in earthen jars. The boats halted and the rowers
swung at the jars with their oars and smashed them.
That was their answer to Dom Manuel, our King.
It's as difficult to cross the seas as it is
to ask the Moors to cross over to Christ.

Note: Pedro Alvares Cabral, with a fleet of thirteen ships and 1200 men, embarked from Portugal on 8 March 1500 for India—a voyage during which he accidentally 'discovered' Brazil, named Vera Cruz by him.

River

In the hills she is hectic
    as downwards from heaven
she descends
on the edge
of the tangled reed-and-sedge
locks of Shiva

in the hills she is loud
    constricted by pelvic rock walls
that indent the un-scanned
    rhythms of her verse

in the hills she talks
to the rocks inside her
smoothens their shoulders
casts her silk over seam and crevice

in the hills she is kingfisher-blue
but she forgets her hue
    moving into the brown bird spray
        over the plains
past the still crocodile
sunning his back
    on mudflats

glacier-born
    the river is love
lets the salmon spawn
    as it moves upstream
in a cyclic and never ending dream

in the plains she reflects:
she has nursed the wanderlust
of lost tribes on her banks
she is perhaps as old as geology, so she forgets
half the earth's dust is her alluvial silt
half of mythology is her alluvial spread

the river is a black mirror at night
    and the quarter moon and the half moon
sail on her and within her by turns—
lamp-lit boats, dream-lit boats
that move with the river's endless dreaming.

Face

he doesn't know her
and he knows
that actually nobody knows anybody.

he doesn't know where she lives
    the unknown is everywhere
distance and perspective
stretch
    from the unknown
    to the unknowable.

he has seen her once
the face hard
as if some resolve had
built a bunker there.

he had seen her face once
and the words blue titanium
had, like the thin winter cry
of a Himalayan thrush,
    suddenly entered his mind.

that grief inhabits her face
    he has sensed
a hard face does not turn soft
but can turn to broken shale.

he wants to say
lady with the broken-shale aura
enclose your darkness,
    this dark enclosure is yours.

    no one can flail or flounder here
but he cannot say it
he does not say it.

Migration 3

we watch rain descend on the flooding river
brown rain on brown river, its muddy ripples
kissing the underbelly of the jumna bridge;
watch hut and shanty, lining the bank,
move to higher perches, higher sandbanks,
that wobble with the damp.
a sack of rained-in rice is moved, a shaggy dog
droops behind the family along with a calf
its halter rope trailing from the neck.

birds are better off moving from the tundra,
eyes closed, map of sky and aerial route embedded
in their genes through ten thousand years of shifting
from arctic blue, ice blue to the green of the warm jheel
to water-nut infested lagoons of the tropics.

as day moves into shadow and a kerosene lamp
flickers somewhere in amazement at its own
audacity, and the family looks at it as at a chimera,
the river migrates to hut and hamlet.

He Is Not Aware

he is not aware
    of the distance
between here and there
the sky means nothing to him, nor
the planet smouldering away each year.
       his world is here
day stares at him like a slab
noon pours red coals on his sweat-pimpled body
    night broods over him
he is grateful for his dreams' desertion
he sleeps like leaves on a sour pond.

time means little to him
hunger is his clock
      he knows noon and nightfall through it.

he has moved from the wilderness of drought
    and its stubble and his village thatch
to arid suburbs, feeding brick kilns,
and then to concrete mixers
      and the city wilderness—
but he doesn't see it as wilderness.

he is not aware
    there is not much distance
between here and there.

She Came

She came
and his pulse quickened.
As on cue
the drizzle-wet breeze
came in through
the window
bringing with it
the rinsed blue
of the rain-washed skies.

She left
and the colour went out of his eyes.

A December Poem

dawn turning opaque on the window glass
crinkling with frost; later the wheeling kite
and the wheel of the year—image
and metaphor mingling in the mind—
these circular meditations could be
the last few for the likes of me.
but I think of the next pothole on the road,
ice-ponds flanking a leaking pipe;
fog like a band across the city's eyes.

there is a time for the oxen and the plough
to mark their furrows, spraying of
hand-held seed, but this is not the time;
a time to watch driftwood moving with the tide;
for photographing black seaweed
draped on a rock, but this is not the time.

there is a time for coffee grounds and tea leaves
but if there's no future, where is the point?
and there's time for an elegy moving
like a slow Wagnerian movement,
but this is not the time.

She Talks of Sheshnag

He slipped in like a premonition you don't believe in;
it had been a long trek, the sweat under my pullover
freezing into crystals, yet the winter never got a sniffle
out of me. An iced fog had erased the road
and the gravel on the bridle track
shivered under my feet as he caught me
halfway through my stumble,
held me a moment longer than he need have.
At the hut, cold made the air thick;
the mirror said my lines were thinly drawn
I combed my wiry hair; the caretaker thought
I was a dirty word libels are all about.
Wrong season, he said, with the abruptness of disapproval;
you've come in the wrong season.

This time, alone with the lake's memory, I came
on a zigzag bar of mist that moved out of the map.
Mother had said you'll move out of your body
but try not to move out of your dreams.
I didn't have to move out of my dream;
no blue can plagiarize the blue of Sheshnag.
Once you admit there are no words for that blue, you are free;
I was free of him, wrong people cross my path
or I, the wrong one, cross theirs.

The mirror again said my lines were thinly drawn,
the wizened caretaker didn't like my stringy hair;
those who disapprove have never learnt to approve
those who see lust in eyes will never see love.
All that he said was 'see the pilgrims to Amarnath
on that hill, when will you join them?' I will not, I said.
The question did not disappear from his eyes;
'I've just come to Sheshnag.' 'For what?'
To negotiate with emptiness.
Then I saw the pilgrim line,
tennis shoes, dhotis, bent spine leaning on a staff
move up like ancestors into limbo.

The Tribal Goddess

I salute her in absentia,
this goddess of the tribes of the forest
of shadows scrimmaging
on the fern floor of the forest
not just the goddess of the dark heart of the forest
but of the forest-fringe
who extends her hand
to meet the vegetal goddess,
protector of those who limp into the forest
the ones who subsist on a diet of nettles,
protector against the lords of the buckshot
and the iron trap, hide-robbers, horn bandits
and ivory thieves

the rational ones continue to despise you
as do the monotheists
who think they are very advanced
and aeons ahead of the polytheists
and the pantheists and solar theists
and lunar- and planet-theists

but as brick forests rise
on concrete plinths and smoke belches forth
coating the sky's lung
we'll be migrating to you
in barefoot trickles at night—always night
in silence or with din
the goddess of nocturnal silence
and the nocturnal howl are the same,
one eye Capricorn and the other Cancer
you'll shortly be in demand
for moss-masked as you are
you are the mother of secrets
goddess of the water springs
still hidden in the earth

A Dam in the Himalayas

Valley floor and flanking hills have gone under.
Roof-tiles are paved flagstones now
and shimmer and refract whenever
a light breeze smears the waters.
The blur that is the temple spire is washed and warped;
it trembles when the waters move.
The palace too has gone down with its veined marble,
—colour of sunsets, burnt sienna—
though its pillars still hold the ceiling
Atlas-like, each pillar
erupting from a carved lotus.

If an underwater flute were activated
its Garhwali melody would gurgle up
in a string of bubbles; and carp and mullet
would scuttle away thinking some water mammoth
on the lake-floor was breathing down their fins.

These are enchanted waters now, mermaid
and water-nymphs, all breast and sinuous waist
move here; flowering trees still drop petals;
kingfisher and blue-jay
sit on an underwater branch looking for prey.

These are not waters, they are mist, memory.
I look for your face, your shadow here,
your body and your bier wrapped in water-weed,
but the waters close in upon
the outlines of your face, now beyond recall,
and mist and vapour rub your smile away.

The Confused Falcon

where would I rather be?
>   move like a dragonfly through high grass
>   live red-eyed through the long sneeze of pollen
>   hear a story about leopard spoor
>   >   leopard cubs
>   >   (hope they are not hungry)

perhaps sight a flamingo alighting on a patch
and take off, finding none of its flock there
hear about a darting pheasant
>   blazing through rushes

as it senses a human footfall behind it

watch an almost-fledgling falcon
>   soar upwards, hover confused

between gravity and an upward draft of air
peering at the gentle curvature
>   of the ground beneath, bewildered,

unable to sort out earth from sky

I would like to walk around
amidst a swirl of thoughts
rummage among half-forgotten images
like someone dazed, dazzled,
half traumatized by light
till dusk is decanted from an amber bottle

tallow-flame nights
>   nights of false consolations.

This Poem Is Going Nowhere Nor Is Life

this string of events that is life
      this string of cells that is the body
      this string of moments that is time
do they ever sit together, have a chat,
come to a sort of a modus vivendi?

does it matter if they don't?
we focus on ourselves, a dream that floated
in last night, the stream of thought
that inhabits us and keeps up its murmur;
grief at finalities, when death and oblivion
take things in their hands, as they always do.
but through its sidereal rounds the earth
    moves at sixty-seven thousand miles per hour;
what are we in front of such phenomena:
    as gravity cracks its whip, planets orbiting,
always in ellipses, remember Kepler (?)
    and comets that keep to their lanes and never honk?
who are we to be obsessed with puny us,
with some frigging feeling that flickers
on a jangled nerve-end?

God said let there be light
instead there was the big bang
am told the guy was startled
'who did this, I wanna know?'
then realization dawned
(there were no dawns till then, mind you
in a gaseous universe—as in political speak—
there can't be any dawns)
this wasn't some kid lighting a fire-cracker!
the universe had gone bust, damn it!

Let's face it
    solace comes with poetry
      a rhyme that clangs against a tin can
insistent, but moves into memory,
        a haiku that flies off a page
      and turns into a bird.

I Wrote a Story

high tide, the breeze strong,
casuarinas leaning on the flanking road
like an arcade of swords over a bridal pair;
road leads to fisher huts in tatters
and the temple on top, ornate and solid
as a civilization that thinks it is forever.
Old man squatting on sand, talking away
to twilight children not knowing they've left.

His angry sons stand behind him:
stealth listening to his wobbling babble,
unhappy at his long hair, one with the wind,
his crablike gait, left knee giving way,
his crab-concerns—he will not step on them,
and the hub and spokes of his mind
gone their separate ways.
They scold him—you are talking to dogs Father
they want bones, not your stories,
why must you invent an absurd one each day?
And he asks what's wrong with a story each day?
All three innocent of the intricate harmony he's in
with tide and tilted casuarinas and crabs
with dusk and salt sprayed over the road.

Prayer on January 30

We won't ask you for the impossible—
to close the hiatus between matter and nothing,
or save the world from a meteor hit.
We don't ask for certitudes, though we know
that the land of nothing-certain is as bad as nothing.
We won't ask you to un-burn
those whose huts and skin have caught fire;
though we may ask for renewal
where the ash has settled.

Let not the harsh winds of our times
blow love away.
Let not the harsh winds of our times
blow our perceptions into a wall
behind which people are sharpening knives.
Let not the harsh dreams of our times
devour us, along with our appetites.
Lead us from this landscape of rubble
to water, but let the sound be real—
even traffic sounds like surf at night.
And let water remain water
and not turn to blood.

Lead us from chemical colours to vegetable dyes,
from plastic to cotton,
from fractions to wholeness.
Ephemeral as we are,
let the infinite touch us somewhere.
Detach us from the tree of time.
And those with no faith,
cast them on the waters of belief.

Let the repressed be brought into light,
the hidden into knowledge.
Let there be harmony
between those who speak of shadows
and those who speak of the sun.

Let the unlit be lit.
Steer the light our way.
Let the forest leaf.
Let the lyric leaf.

Gandhi

You are imprinted on memory
like almost nobody else,
the line drawing that you are,
your round bald head
mirrored in a way
by the rondures of your spectacles.
Later there was that slightly bent back
and the staff-leaning torso.
Naked, knee-down,
I think of your long strides
scissoring a continent
from the black walls of jails
to the white salt of Dandi.

2

That last year must have been terrible for you,
the joy and glory turning to ash in your mouth,
and that tide of blood which darkened many rivers,
though it left your sea at Porbander rather clean.

You walked into flame and arson
and crowds that wielded sharpened steel,
the rim of their eyeballs aflame with hatred.
Sitting comfortably on the sidelines
we thought your cry for peace
was turning into a lightning conductor for war,
and that your plea for ahimsa
was lighting up further fires.
We were wrong, as always—
those who opposed you could never be right.
You walked into the knives of Noakhali
and the blood-dripping lanes of Calcutta.

You knew you were circling
the jagged rim of a volcano,
you, the one voluntary suicide
among a horde of homicides.
You kept inviting death, Mahatma,
till that Godse bullet found you.

Birds and Trees in Iraq

No matter how the desert shuffles between
the two waters
no matter how blood flows in Mesopotamia now
or how the young die with bomb-belts
around their waists
so that the street itself turns into grapeshot.
No matter how many sandbags enclose
nervous machine guns
no matter how the fire engine clangs
and the ambulance screams
dates will sprout and cluster around palm trees
and the kingfisher dressed in lapis lazuli
will float and flutter
over the Tigris
and his warped image will struggle
and shiver in the water.

On a Bed of Rice

If there is terror without
and you huddled in the coils
that define your being
it is best to stay
within your writer's block;
lie there long-haired one
in the cool consoling dark,
twirling the silver bracelet
studded with stones, around
the lustrous brown of your wrists

the walls will dream for you
your glass bangles will speak in the voice
that has got lost in the cavern of your throat
and time and hope will tick
till both get lost in each other,
time fatigued and bored with this endless replication
like rain repeating itself nightlong on a tiled roof

but can someone tell you,
pursed lip, starched dhoti
and shawl dripping from his shoulder
in a waterfall of silk,
to stay within, that region
where light itself turns rickety
as it navigates the smudged glass?
can he ask you to lie there
soundless, your chords un-strummed
numb and immobile?

2

that's where they want you
and how they want you
a cold roast
on a bed of rice.

3

can you write in the dark
won't thought and word balk at scribbling on the walls,
the same glass walls through which
light gets a tremor
as it navigates the outer rim of reality?
move out of the dark doorway and the blind alley
there are no dead ends,
 the planet wide enough for all;
reach out for the open
with your words, but words
will never be enough;
song and slogan and gesture,
make them your friends,
and the clenched fist.

4

and the one who tinkers
with the baroque arabesques of the Zodiac
and slots you in squares
tilted water pot and the
stupid Murakami sheep—forget him.
bustle out of the square into the plaza
don't let them move you back
in rococo time.

5

don't worry about the time to come
and the time gone.
aren't the past and the future
all the same
just pages to write upon?

Orpheus and Persephone

The Guard* to Creon

 (*From Antigone*)

There was no gash on the earth where he had lain
no dent made by pickaxe or shovel
no mark left by wagon wheel as it trundled here.
The night watch and the day watch were both confused;
we rubbed our eyes, we can't even say
that his body turned to mist, for mist and fog
are palpable, disappearance is not.
We accused each other but no one had connived
at the burial rites—your orders were so strict
death awaited whoever buried him.

Then it emerged from under a sheet of dust
so fine it looked like pollen, as if the wind
had covered her child and given it burial;
for we reasoned only the wind gods could defy
the King's severe edict without peril.
The body bore no beak-mark of carrion bird,
nor indentations of vulpine teeth.
We are not at fault, night watch nor day watch.
The wind has done it Lord, and who can know
the temper of the wind's mind?
The body was clammy as if night dews
had left their funeral libations on the corpse.
If you are hunting the guilty, Creon
we the guards could tell you whom to target:
look out for the night dews and the night wind.

―――――――――――――

*Reporting the attempted burial of Polyneices

Tiresias to Creon

To the omen-altar and the augury seat
where birds foregather, I went, led neither
by tapping stick nor helper—a blind man's friends,
but drawn there by the clamour of birds.
There was much screeching and anger in them;
that beak and talon were in great use was clear
even to the eyeless, even to Tiresias.

Divination descends from the gods on high
through the skies to the birds in the sky
till it passes on to unfortunates like me.
An oracle is an oracle, though he doesn't know
who speaks through his tongue or sees through his eye.
I cannot see the sacrifices but am told
liver and entrails speak of disaster.
I cannot see the altar flames but I am sure
their chameleon colours mutated
each moment from red to blue to lambent green,
even as the altar-fires were lit.
But I can see the black wall of night descend on day.

Sickness has already dawned on us, Creon
though you cannot see that dawn. Be warned
the gods are angry that dog and glutted bird
are gorging on Polyneices, who lies
open to sky and sky-bird and beasts of the earth.
Bend your knee to the dead, let prayer and incense,
ceremony and rite cloak the fallen.

Afterthought at Thebes

Darkening with blood and battle-burn
the streets are all set to write his epitaph,
when the postern gate, left unguarded
lets the Macedonians in.
Then the stampede at the Electra Gate
and all is lost.
Still the Thebans die where they stand, fighting,
flailing away with their bare hands
or with the hafts of broken javelins.

The city of prophecies
the city of the blind
the city of Tiresias and Oedipus
now lies at his feet.
As the temple gates are forced open and plundered
and thighs forced open and the women violated,
Alexander says,
'Let the city be razed
and the people enslaved and sold.'

Then the afterthought:
'But spare the descendants of Pindar
—also his house.'
And scribes grovel
and chronicles glow
about his flaming generosity
and millenniums remember him
for this aesthetic touch.

Greek Vases

On their red-and-black vases and their amphorae,
the equatorial bulge of their amphorae,
are spearmen setting out, one of them
about to climb onto a one-horse chariot.
When soldiers move one knows their travel plans—
long sapping marches through scrub and marsh,
and deserts from where the oases have fled;
till one windy night they come upon an escarpment
overlooking a plain embered with campfires,
Trojan or Turk or Persian
and know in the pith of their hearts
that the next dawn means enemy horse and steel.

But we are circling black vase and amphora
and find the spearmen clad in armour
and their spears etched
on the baked memory of clay—
spears longer than the lines of Homer
or the chronicle of Callisthenes.
Behind them are tearful women—
wives and mothers always in black,
as if already in mourning.

Lament and prophecy:
Trojan women, Andromache and Cassandra,
clamber on to the vase without being there.

Orpheus and Persephone

He couldn't wait, winter was upon him.
Through abyss and tunnel he had to go down
to meet her in the seed-dark of the underworld—
she in her iceberg aspect, face frosted in a frown,

or so he imagined. He couldn't wait
for spring when she trod the earth again and turned
her face towards the sun like a heliotrope.
Placental seed would pine for her return

and all vegetation which she quickened into life.
He hadn't planned, should he on bended knee
ask another lease for his snake-stung wife?

How are the dead retrieved? Retrieve, was that the word?
Ask for her soul, or the rest—limbs, hair, laughter, voice?
Give me a hearing Goddess! He thought she hadn't heard.

2

Halfway through his subterranean voyage he froze.
That river was blacker than a starless night,
driftwood-river clogged with driftwood-souls,
and Charon paddling away—Goddess help! He cried.

Is this a river or black despair that I see?
There's such silence here as I never heard.
Heard? Is that how silence sinks into your system?
What state am I in, floundering around a word?

He berates himself (his confidence has vanished)
he needs a drink, (there's none to be had.)
Think of her as exile, think of her as banished.

Switch the states, exile and death, think of the soul
as émigré. Unsure of himself, he has no one to speak to.
He could talk to his lyre—it would sing as told.

3

(Persephone Awaits him)

His music had come to her as rumour,
and even rumour rang like a silver bell!
Now he's on his way, past windbreak, corn-stubble
to this dank cavernous space men call Hades, Hell.

'He has lowered himself onto our river Styx!'
News of him comes every minute to her throne.
She claps for her younger maids to comb her hair,
laquer her toenails, throws out the older crones.

For once the dark smothers her, she notes with surprise.
'Let candles and the flambeaux be lit! Things here
are dark as dreams yet to travel to the eyes.'

She stills her excitement, but the maids are too far gone.
'We've heard him!' they cry. 'His music is magic,
we don't know if he has a lyre or a wand.'

4

The fire of anticipation threads her gut.
She's heard so much and the stories were long—
he raised a hill sloping to heaven with one note,
he could pour the night, all the stars in one song;

the spheres and their music were just his lyre's echo.
Birds of the air and beasts of the wild were tamed
by this son of Calliope. And when
he was in sorrow his music was like rain.

Intuitively she knows what he would ask for:
Eurydice to walk the world once again,
and sadly she would have to turn him down,

but with philosophy's salve, she'd keep him on track—
death was renunciation of life he would be told,
and what you renounce can't be taken back.

5

Frozen-flat he thought the place would be—windless, lightless,
a country of black mist bordering Night.
He found silver pillars holding up black marble roof;
a dark shimmer about it could pass off for light.

He caressed his lyre strings, 'Goddess of the dark,
Persephone I've dropped a thousand floors
to reach you, beseech you, have travelled your great river,
that is how suppliants come to your door.

Goddess of seedlings, you who live in the earth's black core
there can be no secrets from you—you are secrecy itself.
Surely you know what I am here for.'

She understood of course, nodded in assent;
had heard the first gust of his lyre's melody and wished
his music wouldn't move into lament.

6

He played on and Persephone said
we take our bearings from rivers—Styx, lithe Lethe.
I got half drowsed by your gentler strains, and loved it,
sleep after all is a tributary of death.

But melancholy grimes your face and your melodies.
You carry a dark cloud and who knows when it rains?
Your lyre suddenly brings nightfall even here,
in this dark country where only night remains

in perpetual tenantry. I admire you greatly
but your angry strains could burn pastures, vistas.
Those who love desperately mourn desperately.

So take Eurydice with you, you can backtrack
to the world you came from. Forget her sojourn here,
think only of the future—AND DON'T LOOK BACK!

Luxor Diary

Small Truths

Small truths need to be so small
that they are lost among larger things
which have no truck with truth.

Once the plague gets hold of you,
introductions become difficult.
You need royalty to usher you in;
never mind the place,
never mind the company.

He has to meet the gods
of subterranean regions—
the passageway is secret,
secrecy is another name for darkness.
When you go down
you need a pine torch
you need an incense burner.

When your son has embarked,
start your preparations—
Wraps, jars—
and ask the lord of the hieroglyph
to be ready with his quill.

Rameses III

They meet as equals always,
the Pharaoh and the gods.
Rameses has the boldness to slide
one arm around the waist of Isis,
goddess of magic and kindness,
healing and motherhood,
Isis in her glory, the moon-disc
caught between her horns.

Then he introduces his son
to the hereafter—
the hereafter with its own physics
and its own geology.
Meet the gate-keeper god,
the dog-headed Thoth.
Meet Ptah, he says, the keeper of souls,
in a way, the god of death.

Here too they are equals, except
he meets them with incense-burners,
while his young son, caught
by plague in Thebes,
carries a torch.

When it's his own turn
to meet the mortuary gods,
Rameses knows he'll need them:
flame and pine-torch, incense
         and incense-burner.

The Ibis-god

The ibis draws his lines
as he pecks at grain—
a string of dot and dash
that moves on the ground
in geometric perfection.
When the scribes saw this they said
'He is the lord of the written word,
and hence of learning!'
And where was learning more needed
than near the faultlines of the underworld?
So Thoth, the Ibis-god
became the god of death.

***

Footnote

At the Luxor temple they met
the Nile-god and Rameses.
The papyrus of upper Egypt
and the lotus of the lower
are both yours now
     says the Nile-god Habie.

And beneath them a single rope
drawn across the necks
of a phalanx of slaves—
a Libyan from the desert
a Nubian from the fifth cataract,
each dark and strong-thewed
and handsome as Rameses himself.

Under the celebration
the footnote of sorrow.

The Temple to Hathor

When you want peace
you send emissaries.
What Queen Hathshepsut sent
to the nation of Punt
were bead necklaces
and gold bracelets,
large enough to fit
the elephantiasis-stricken Queen
of that far land.
The King of Punt, turbaned
and large-bellied and black
like some trader from a bazaar
in Madagascar, raised his hand
in blessing and peace, giving
panther skins and ivory in return.

But Hathshepsut had wanted
henna for her hair, and incense.
The King of Punt gave whole incense trees.
'Take them if you can carry them.'
All this on the walls, painted
in oxidized colours.

There is drama on the walls as well,
a drama of erasures,
as incense urns are offered
to the gentle cow goddess, Hathor.
But where is Hathshepsut?
She's been wiped out.
The great Thutmose, who murdered her—
you are bound to be great if you murder
the only queen Egypt had before Cleopatra—
wanted her out of her own temple.

To preempt her reincarnation,
to make the hereafter itself short-lived
a sure shot method was
to erase her from each fresco.
So Thutmose ravaged her tomb
and smashed the canopic jars
that contained her entrails
and destroyed her cartouche.

As Hathor and Anubis
accept their incense urns
the suppliant queen lives by her absence.

And yet,
   with the soapstone hills
      as backdrop,
         through terrace and ramp
            the temple flows down like a cataract.

Translations from Faiz Ahmed Faiz

The Sad City

(Yeh sheher udas itna zyada toh nahin tha)

Though everyone didn't own a bar or plenty's horn
this city was never so melancholy and forlorn.

Two or three loonies roamed the by-lanes, lost
but their garments were not hundred-patched or torn.

Love's wayfarer not spotting his love!
Simpleton though he be, he was not that lovelorn.

Fatigued momentarily one day the eyelids closed
to sleep and not wake up—that was never on.

This city was never so melancholy and forlorn.

A Ghazal in the Memory of Makhdoom

Moonlight Troubled Me the Long Night
(Chandani dil dukhaati rahi raat bhar)

Your memories kept flowing in night long
Moonlight kept troubling my heart night long.

Flaming at times and guttering on occasions
The candle, it kept flickering night long.

A perfume kept changing its garments
A picture broke into unbroken song night long.

Under the shadow of a flower-decked plate
The nightingale narrated a saga night long.

For one who didn't come, even the door chain
Clank-called for him night long.

The heart kept beat with one solitary hope
The torch of desire troubled me night long.

Quatrains

Night found your lost memories and swept them in
Like spring alighting on scrub by stealth
Like the stir and rustle of cool desert winds,
Like a fevered brow cooling to sudden health.

***

In black despair I find myself drowned
The heart is just a heart, it is often down
You gifted me a sorrow and forgot your gift
I remain so obliged, it weighs me down.

***

Sadness gets sprayed over the seasons of the heart
Melancholy clings to life till the end
Betrayal is what flesh and nature yearn for
Even as this dawns on you, youth is already spent.

***

Don't indulge so much today that you can't face the morrow
Or that night which is not the night of your black tresses
This desire is an entity by itself
But love is not all about desire and caresses.

***

What if quill and tablet have been impounded?
I have dipped my fingers in my heart's blood and pain
What if the tongue is sealed? I have kept
A tongue in each link of my iron chains.

Acknowledgements

Many thanks to Arundhathi Subramaniam for taking the time and making the effort to write the introduction. I am grateful.

The poems in this collection have not appeared in any of my earlier volumes, though they have figured in a few journals and anthologies. I regret to say that I cannot remember all the publications where these poems have appeared. The ones I recall appeared as follows:

'In Night Country' in *Acumen*, UK.

'Some Poems for Akhmatova' have been accepted for the book *What is Time?: An Anthology of Contemporary Indian Writing* (Red Hen Press, USA).

'Cabral' and 'Greek Vases' in *Wasafiri*, London.

'Cranes' in *Kindness: Uddartha–Australia-India Cultural Exchange Volume* (2012).

'Barbet' in *The Indian Quarterly*.

'This Poem is Going Nowhere' in *Bengal Lights*, Dhaka.

'River' appeared in the book *The Golden Boat: River Poems* (Yoda Press)

'Luxor Diary' in *The Poetry Review*, London.

'Patna to Nalanda' in *Re-Markings Special Number: A World Assembly of Poets*.

ALSO IN POETRY BY SPEAKING TIGER

AVAILABLE LIGHT
NEW AND COLLECTED POEMS

C.P. Surendran

'C.P. Surendran bears witness to...what James Agee memorably described as "the cruel radiance of what is". Anyone who looks directly at that "cruel radiance" is very likely to be wounded; for the poet is not only a pilgrim in a dangerous landscape but also a trespasser in secluded zones, psychic, cultural or political, that would prefer to guard their mysteries. As in Greek mythology, the guardian of such a sanctuary, usually a serpent or a dragon, inflicts a wound on the trespasser who has entered and violated the temenos. It is the wound of unbearable knowledge....It is a sacred wound, and poetry, certainly for C.P. Surendran, is an attempted suture for this sacred wound.'

—Ranjit Hoskote

ALSO IN POETRY BY SPEAKING TIGER

FULL DISCLOSURE
NEW AND COLLECTED POEMS (1981-2017)

Manohar Shetty

'Here is a book worth celebrating: Manohar Shetty's *Full Disclosure: New and Collected Poems (1981–2017)*, which gathers more than thirty years of work from a major voice in world Anglophone poetry. More accurately, this book presents a range of voices—in some of the multi-sectioned poems a choir—as Shetty writes through a variety of personae and perspectives, delivering emotionally resonant deep imagery and intellectual precision, profound compassion and ironic wit, in equal parts.... This collection provides us with a broad survey of a celebrated poet's past and present while offering an enticement for his—and our—future.'

—John Hennessy,
poetry editor of *The Common*

ALSO IN POETRY BY SPEAKING TIGER

NEW DELHI LOVE SONGS

Michael Creighton

'New Delhi Love Songs is a collection abounding with shakarkandiwalas, jasmine-sellers, FM radios and cyclists, the Ghaziabad flower market and Moolchand flyover; the Delhi all around us, the Delhi of "your flesh, your seeds, / your skin", of "sweat and soil / mixed with clover, sun and wind". Unusual, deeply affecting in their attentiveness to life that seldom makes headlines, these poems reinforce the skeins of humanity that sustain us. They are tender and droll—two qualities we desperately need, in the capital but also elsewhere—yet steadfast in their eschewal of easy sentimentality and facile observations. New Delhi Love Songs makes the heart ache; but also sing, from time to time, for this is where "even a dead river looks lovely".'

—Karthika Nair

ALSO IN POETRY BY SPEAKING TIGER

NINE: POEMS

Anupama Raju

A debut collection of poems by an acclaimed young poet.

'Urgent and passionate, these poems circle age-old preoccupations of love and longing. This is perilous terrain where the danger of cliché lurks at every turn. However, without resorting to the easy distancing strategies of irony, the poet plunges into psychologically fraught zones of "poetry, perfidy and Pandora", ready to give voice to the vulnerability and confusion attendant on such an exploration. A quiet blend of authenticity and artistry sees her through, transforming familiar tropes of blood and longing, pain and death, into the "burnt letters" of warm, pulsating verse. Anupama Raju cuts close to the bone in this debut collection of poems.'

—Arundhathi Subramaniam

ALSO IN POETRY BY SPEAKING TIGER

THE SAND LIBRARIES OF TIMBUKTU

Rohinton Daruwala

'Rohinton Daruwala's poems unfold like a baramasa, an almanac of seasons and sensations, exquisite torments and explosions of delight. He essays a sensuous portraiture of place, invoking torrential monsoons, arid summers, railway bridges at night, libraries in deserts. [He] spells out a frank eroticism in the textures and flavours of fruit...at the same time, [he] is entangled in the hypermodern present. He gathers traces of the loved one from residues both material and digital... [He] maps the city, not only through the portraiture of human protagonists, but also through the micro-ecologies inhabited by butterflies and sparrows... In Daruwala's handling, the poem can be an oblique parable, a brief lamp of wisdom in the wind of distraction: light as breath, yet as essential.'

—Ranjit Hoskote

www.ingramcontent.com/pod-product-compliance
Lightning Source LLC
Chambersburg PA
CBHW070309240426
43663CB00039BA/2546